HUMAN BODY

A NATURE-FACT BOOK

by
D.J. Arneson

Illustrated by
Howard S. Friedman

Copyright © 1991 Kidsbooks, Inc.
7004 California Ave.
Chicago, IL 60645

ISBN: 1-56156-024-3

Manufactured in the United States of America

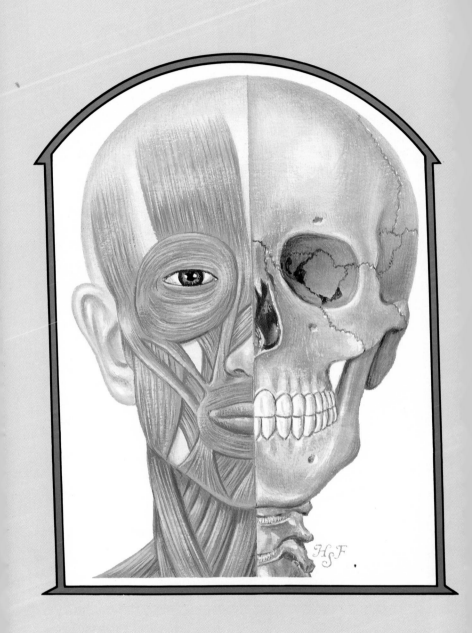

THE HUMAN BODY

Imagine you're in a park. You hear someone shout, "Wild throw!" You turn in time to see a red rubber ball coming your way. You run toward it as fast as you can. You trip, but quickly regain your balance. The ball drops into your hands. "I've got it!" you say, puffing to catch your breath. "Nice catch," the voice says. You smile.

Your body does many things all at once. You can hear, see, think, move, and breathe. You also grow, understand, digest, sweat, remember, heal, fight infection, store energy, and get rid of wastes. You're a boy or a girl and you're made of many parts and systems.

Systems are groups of specialized parts. All of your body's parts and systems work together. Most are *involuntary*—they work automatically. You don't have to tell your heart to pump blood, for example. Others, like moving your arm or wiggling your nose, are *voluntary*—they are under your control to start or stop when you want.

All parts and systems are made of tiny *cells*, the body's building blocks. They are so small that a row of 2,500 cells would be just one inch long. There are many kinds of cells and each does a different job. There are hair cells, skin cells, muscle cells, nerves cells, blood cells, and many others.

Over 50 *million* cells die every second! Fortunately, just as many new cells are made to replace them. Nerve cells are not replaced. A very old person has about 25 percent fewer nerve cells than you do.

Knowing how your body works helps to keep it healthy.

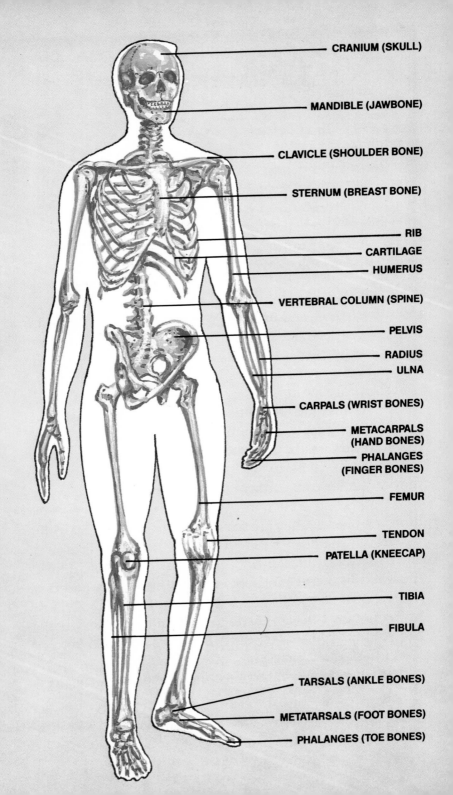

CRANIUM (SKULL)

MANDIBLE (JAWBONE)

CLAVICLE (SHOULDER BONE)

STERNUM (BREAST BONE)

RIB

CARTILAGE

HUMERUS

VERTEBRAL COLUMN (SPINE)

PELVIS

RADIUS

ULNA

CARPALS (WRIST BONES)

METACARPALS
(HAND BONES)

PHALANGES
(FINGER BONES)

FEMUR

TENDON

PATELLA (KNEECAP)

TIBIA

FIBULA

TARSALS (ANKLE BONES)

METATARSALS (FOOT BONES)

PHALANGES (TOE BONES)

THE SKELETAL SYSTEM

Your *skeleton* is made of bones. It is like the steel girders that support a tall building. Without a frame, the building would collapse. Without a skeleton, you could not sit, stand, or even move.

Bones give your body its basic shape. They support you and protect vital organs like your brain, heart, and lungs from injury. Bones also anchor muscles so you can move.

There are 206 bones in an adult human body. The largest is the *femur* or "thigh bone." It is long, thick, heavy, and very strong and requires the body's largest muscles to move it. The smallest are three tiny bones in the inner ear which are so delicate they can be moved by a whisper.

Bones are made mostly of *calcium*, a mineral that is essential to good health. The outside of a bone is hard and dense, but inside is a spongy material filled with blood vessels and nerves called *marrow*. Marrow makes red and white blood cells.

Bones are joined by elastic tissue called *ligament* which acts like a hinge so the bones can move. Bone ends are covered with *cartilage,* a soft tissue that protects joints from shock.

There are almost as many bones in your hands and feet as there are in the rest of your body. There are seven bones in your neck, the same as in a giraffe's neck. The top of your skull is about as thick as a pencil eraser is wide. Your temples are only half that thick.

Your bones will keep growing until you are about 20 years old. The bones of a person who does not get enough calcium in his or her diet will grow weak and brittle with age. Proper diet and exercise will help to keep them strong.

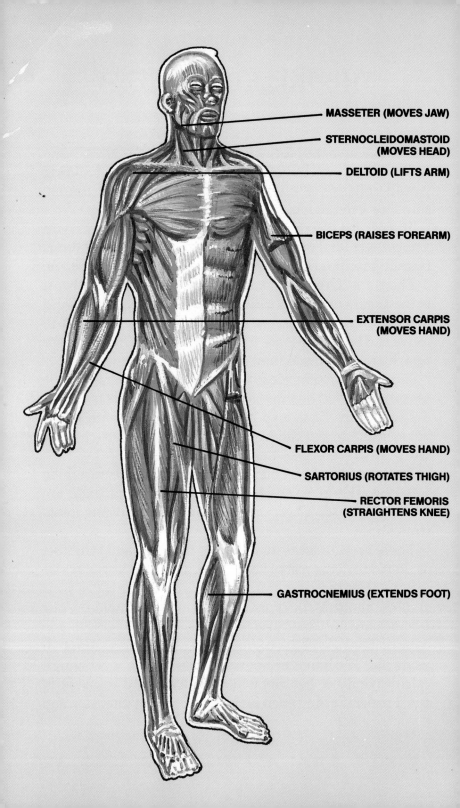

MASSETER (MOVES JAW)

STERNOCLEIDOMASTOID (MOVES HEAD)

DELTOID (LIFTS ARM)

BICEPS (RAISES FOREARM)

EXTENSOR CARPIS (MOVES HAND)

FLEXOR CARPIS (MOVES HAND)

SARTORIUS (ROTATES THIGH)

RECTOR FEMORIS (STRAIGHTENS KNEE)

GASTROCNEMIUS (EXTENDS FOOT)

THE MUSCULAR SYSTEM

Muscles are your body's "motors." They move bones and organs by contracting (getting shorter). You have over 600 muscles. About 35 to 40 percent of your weight is muscle.

Muscle is made of rows of thread-like cells. Some muscle cells are a few inches long. When muscle cells contract, the muscle shortens. If the muscle is connected to a bone, the bone moves. If the muscle surrounds a space like the heart or the intestines, the space is squeezed smaller and anything in it is forced to move, like toothpaste squeezed in a tube.

Skeletal muscles move bones and certain organs like the eyes and tongue. It also encloses and protects the abdominal organs. Skeletal muscle is attached to bone by tendons, a strong, elastic tissue. Skeletal muscle is voluntary.

Smooth muscle is involuntary. The smooth muscles of your heart, blood vessels, and intestines, for example, work by themselves.

Cardiac muscle is a specialized muscle found only in the heart. It also works automatically.

Muscles don't push, they only pull. When you push something, you are really pulling bones. The bones "push" because they are levers. If you could use all your muscles to pull in one direction at the same time, you could lift over 25 tons. Muscles can support 1,000 times their own weight.

Your largest muscle is big enough to sit on, and you do. It is the muscle that moves your thigh. Your smallest is so small it fits in your inner ear where it moves a tiny bone associated with hearing.

You use 17 different muscles to smile, but it takes 43 muscles to make a frown.

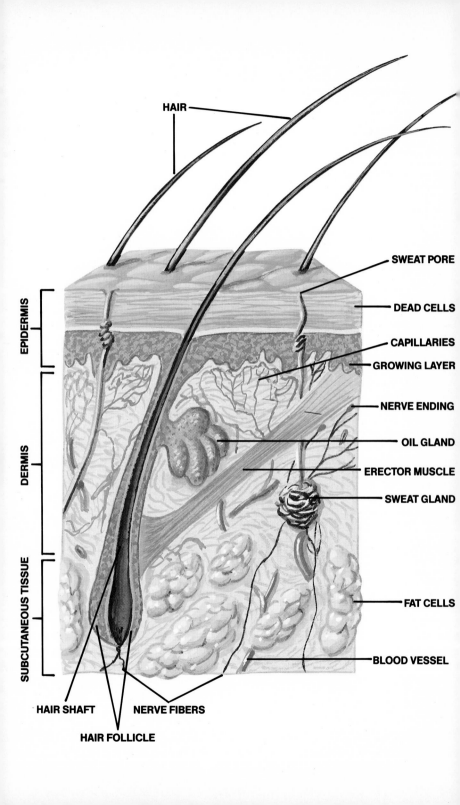

HAIR

SWEAT PORE

DEAD CELLS

EPIDERMIS

CAPILLARIES

GROWING LAYER

NERVE ENDING

OIL GLAND

DERMIS

ERECTOR MUSCLE

SWEAT GLAND

SUBCUTANEOUS TISSUE

FAT CELLS

BLOOD VESSEL

HAIR SHAFT

NERVE FIBERS

HAIR FOLLICLE

THE SKIN

The *skin* is the body's largest organ. It covers the body to keep out bacteria and harmful substances and prevents tissues from drying out. It helps to regulate body temperature. The skin also eliminates certain wastes through sweating and makes vitamin D from sunlight. Skin thickness depends on its use. The soles of the hands and feet are three times thicker than eyelid skin, for example.

The outer layer of the skin is the *epidermis*. It is made of cells that grow deep inside the skin and are pushed to the surface where they die. As the dead cells wear off, they are replaced by others.

The deepest layer of the epidermis contains cells that produce *melanin*, a substance that gives skin color. Freckles are tiny patches of melanin.

The *dermis*, or "true skin," is under the epidermis. It contains elastic connective tissue, blood vessels, and nerves. Sweat glands, oil glands, and hair and nails grow in the dermis and *subcutaneous* layer which is under the dermis. The subcutaneous layer contains fat cells that act as insulation and can be burned by the body for energy.

Sweat glands pass *perspiration* (water and mineral wastes) onto the skin through tiny pores to cool the body through evaporation. An adult has about 2 million sweat glands. *Sebum*, an oily substance from oil glands, keeps hair soft.

A person weighing 70 pounds has about 10 pounds of skin. A square inch of skin on the back of your hand has about 40 hairs, about 4 yards of blood vessels, and about 17 yards of nerves. Each hair in the skin has a tiny muscle. When the muscle contracts, the hair stands up to make a "goose-bump."

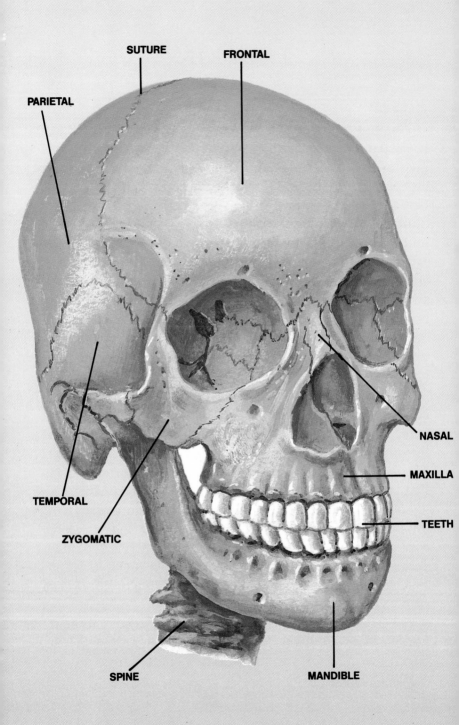

SUTURE

FRONTAL

PARIETAL

NASAL

MAXILLA

TEETH

TEMPORAL

ZYGOMATIC

SPINE

MANDIBLE

THE SKULL

The *skull* has 21 bones tightly joined to protect the brain and other organs inside, and one, the jawbone, that moves. The *cranium* holds the brain. It has 8 bones. The facial bones, 14 in all, form the face. The organs of sight (eyes), hearing (ears), balance (inner ears), and taste and smell (tongue and nose) are in the skull. Hollow spaces called *sinuses* in some skull bones reduce the skull's weight without losing strength. They also act as "echo chambers" and help to give your voice its distinctive sound.

The skull sits on top of the *vertebral column* (spine) and is held in place by muscles that allow it to turn in many directions. The base of the skull has holes for the spinal cord, nerves, and blood vessels to enter. The throat does not enter the skull, but is connected to the mouth cavity by soft tissue.

The front of the skull has openings to hold the eyes which are connected to the brain by a nerve that goes through a smaller hole behind each eye. Two side-by-side openings, the *nasal cavities*, connect the inside of the nose to the throat. Small holes on each side of the skull connect the outer ears with the inner ears.

The bones at the top of a baby's skull are soft until the child is about 2 years old.

The skull has many bumps and ridges for the attachment of muscles.

The temples, areas on the sides of the skull between the eyes and ears, are thin compared to the top of the skull. A blow to the temple can be very dangerous.

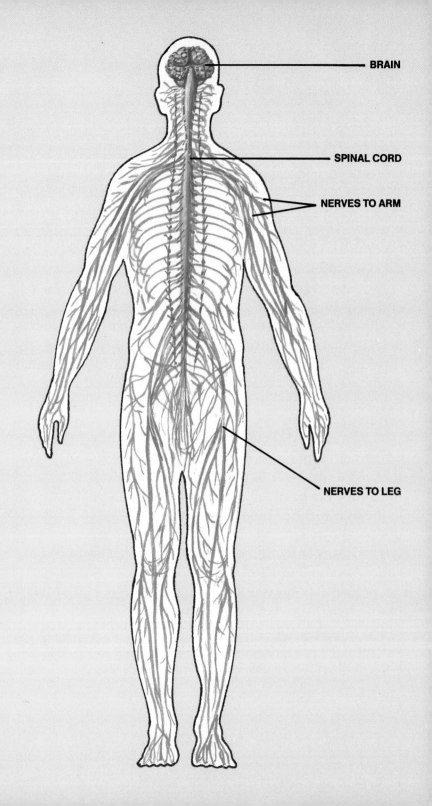

BRAIN

SPINAL CORD

NERVES TO ARM

NERVES TO LEG

THE NERVOUS SYSTEM

The brain, spinal cord, and nerves make up the *nervous system*, your body's control and communication network. The nervous system links all your body systems so they can work together properly. It is also your connection with the outside world through your sensory organs.

Your brain is your master control center. Different areas of the brain have different jobs. You think with the area just behind your forehead. You understand sound with the areas above your ears and vision is interpreted at the back of your head. Almost everything you do is controlled by a specific area of your brain. Some actions, like catching a ball, require thinking. Others, like breathing or heartbeat, are automatic.

Nerves are long threads of specialized cells that connect all parts of your body to your brain. There are almost 45 miles of nerves in your body. They are connected to sensitive nerve cells in your eyes, ears, skin, nose, and other organs. Nerve cells sense light, sound, heat or cold, pressure, and smell and send electrical messages to the brain. Messages to and from your brain travel up to 250 miles per hour along nerves as electricity. When you catch a ball, nerves in your hand send a message through other nerves to the spinal cord and then to the brain. A return message tells your finger muscles to close your hand around the ball.

The brain's surface is wrinkled. If it were smooth and flat, it would cover a dining room table. A brain's size is not a sign of intelligence.

An average adult brain weighs about 48 ounces, or about as much as a large, ripe cantaloupe.

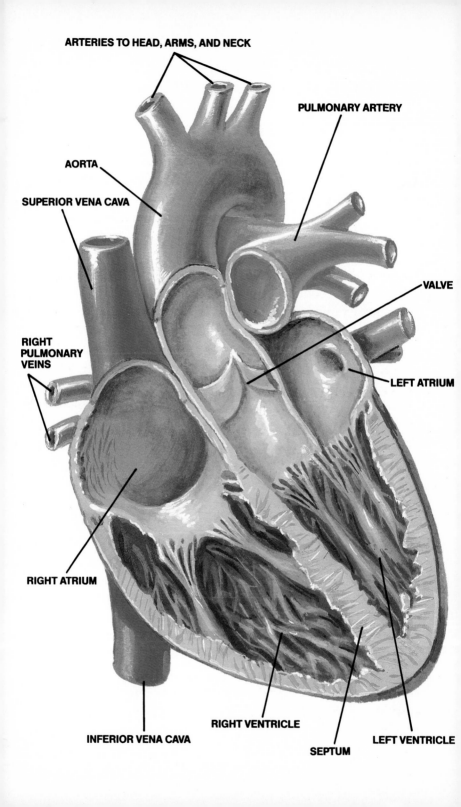

ARTERIES TO HEAD, ARMS, AND NECK

PULMONARY ARTERY

AORTA

SUPERIOR VENA CAVA

VALVE

RIGHT PULMONARY VEINS

LEFT ATRIUM

RIGHT ATRIUM

INFERIOR VENA CAVA

RIGHT VENTRICLE

SEPTUM

LEFT VENTRICLE

THE HEART

Your *heart* is a muscular pump slightly larger than a fist. It is located between your lungs, just to the left of your breastbone. Its job is to force blood through your circulatory system. It began beating before you were born. It will beat about 72 times a minute for your whole life. That is about two and a half billion times. In one year it will circulate about 650,000 gallons of blood, enough to fill 52 average swimming pools.

The heart is really two pumps, one on either side, divided by a partition down the middle. Each pump beats separately ("thump-thump"). Each side has two chambers, an *atrium* on top and a *ventricle* below. The chambers have one-way valves that prevent blood from flowing the wrong direction. When a chamber contracts, its entrance valve closes and its exit valve opens.

The right atrium receives blood returning from the body. The right side "thump" sends the blood into the right ventricle. Blood in the right ventricle is pumped to the lungs. The blood already in the lungs is forced back to the heart, into the left atrium. From there it goes to the left ventricle where the left-side "thump" pumps it through the body. The heart rests between beats.

Blood circulates through the whole body in about one minute. It travels about ten miles per hour which is about as fast as a bee can fly.

The heartbeat is automatically controlled by the nervous system which monitors the body's need for oxygen. Running causes the heart to beat faster. The heart has its own blood supply. A "heart attack" occurs when the heart's blood supply is interrupted and heart muscle dies.

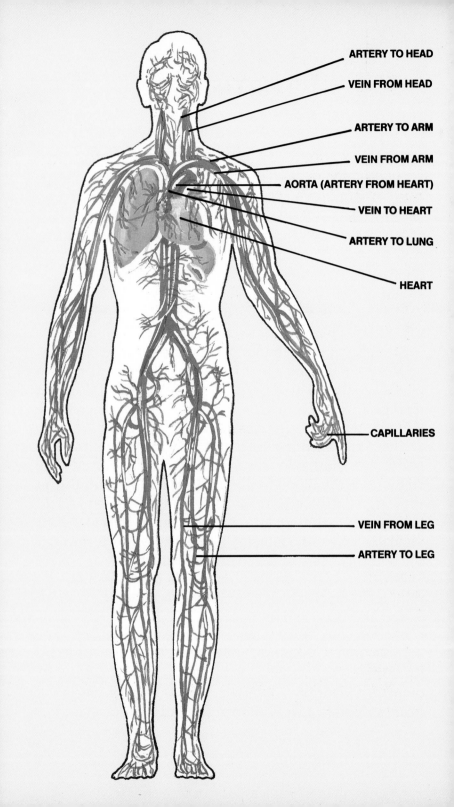

ARTERY TO HEAD

VEIN FROM HEAD

ARTERY TO ARM

VEIN FROM ARM

AORTA (ARTERY FROM HEART)

VEIN TO HEART

ARTERY TO LUNG

HEART

CAPILLARIES

VEIN FROM LEG

ARTERY TO LEG

THE CIRCULATORY SYSTEM

Your *circulatory system* consists of your heart and a closed system of small tubes called *blood vessels* for transporting blood to all parts of the body. "Closed" means the blood does not get out unless a vessel's wall is damaged. End to end, the network of blood vessels would circle the world over two times.

Blood vessels are grouped by what they do. *Arteries* carry oxygen-rich blood from the heart to other parts of the body. The largest artery is about one inch in diameter. *Veins* carry blood from the body back to the heart. *Capillaries* carry blood from small arteries to body cells and return it to small veins.

Capillaries are microscopically small tubes narrower than a human hair, with walls only one cell thick. Nutrients, hormones, and oxygen carried by the blood pass through the walls into a slightly salty fluid that surrounds all living body cells. Blood stays in the capillaries. The cells absorb the materials they need. Cell wastes pass into the solution and through the capillary walls into the bloodstream which carries them to the lungs, kidneys, skin, and other organs for excretion.

Blood is made of *plasma*, a liquid that is 90 percent water, and *corpuscles*, which are specialized cells. Red blood cells carry oxygen. Blood in arteries is bright red because it is rich in oxygen. Blood in veins has a bluish color. White cells fight infection by destroying disease-causing organisms. *Platelets* are cell fragments that prevent bleeding by causing blood to clot.

A 90-pound boy or girl has about three quarts of blood in his or her circulatory system.

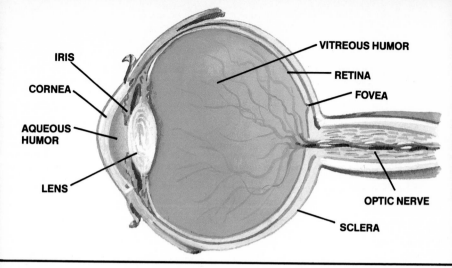

- IRIS
- CORNEA
- AQUEOUS HUMOR
- LENS
- VITREOUS HUMOR
- RETINA
- FOVEA
- OPTIC NERVE
- SCLERA

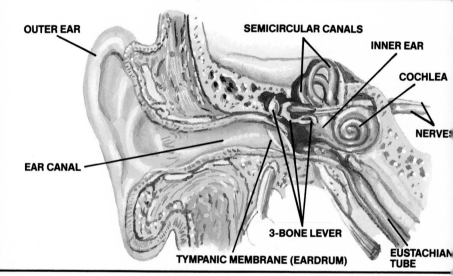

- OUTER EAR
- SEMICIRCULAR CANALS
- INNER EAR
- COCHLEA
- NERVES
- EAR CANAL
- 3-BONE LEVER
- TYMPANIC MEMBRANE (EARDRUM)
- EUSTACHIAN TUBE

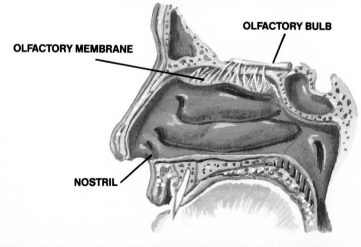

- OLFACTORY BULB
- OLFACTORY MEMBRANE
- NOSTRIL

THE SENSORY ORGANS

You see, hear, smell, taste, and feel the world around you and even catch your balance using sensory information received through your eyes, ears, nose, tongue, and skin.

You see when light reflected off an object enters your eyes through a lens in the pupil and is focused on the *retina* at the back of your eyeballs. Nerve endings in the retina sense the light and change the sensations into electrical signals. The signals travel over the optic nerve to the brain where they are translated into images.

The retina is about as thick as a sheet of paper. It is about the size of a postage stamp and has 130 million cells.

When sound waves in the air beat against your ear drums, they are converted to motion. The motion travels over tiny bones in the inner ear to chambers filled with liquid. Nerves change the motion into signals for the brain to "hear" as sound. Humans can distinguish about 400,000 different sounds. The brain also translates movement of the liquid so you can keep your balance. You feel dizzy when the liquid is moving while you are standing still.

Tiny particles of material enter your nose when you breath. They touch specialized nerves in the nose that produce messages which the brain interprets as smell. Smell is closely associated with taste. Cells on the tongue called *taste buds* sense sweet, sour, salty, and bitter tastes.

Nerve endings in your skin and other parts of your body are sensitive to heat and cold, pressure, and pain. Depending on their specialty, they send signals to the brain that are translated according to what caused them. An ice cube feels cold. A feather tickles. A scratch can be painful.

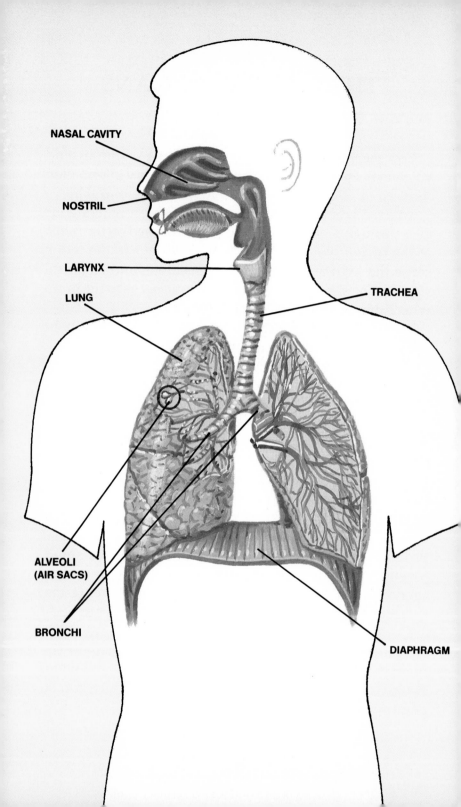

NASAL CAVITY

NOSTRIL

LARYNX

TRACHEA

LUNG

ALVEOLI
(AIR SACS)

BRONCHI

DIAPHRAGM

THE RESPIRATORY SYSTEM

Your breathing speeds up when you run, your muscles work harder, and your blood circulates faster because your body needs more oxygen. The job of your *respiratory system* is to get oxygen to your blood and remove carbon dioxide from it.

Air enters and leaves the respiratory system when you breathe. A child breathes from 20 to 40 times a minute. Adults breathe from 12 to 20 times a minute. Oxygen-rich air is pulled into your nose when you inhale. It goes down your *trachea* (windpipe) and enters your lungs inside your chest. If all the tissue in your lungs were flat, like a sheet, it would cover a tennis court.

In the lungs, branch-like *bronchi* (air tubes) carry the air to over 3 million tiny *alveoli* (air sacs). Blood-filled capillaries in the air sacs exchange oxygen and carbon dioxide. The blood returns to the heart which pumps it throughout the body. The waste-laden air is exhaled into the atmosphere.

A dome-shaped sheet of muscle, the *diaphragm*, separates the chest cavity from the abdominal cavity. When you inhale, the diaphragm contracts downward and the chest walls expand. The chest cavity gets larger. Air rushes into the lungs because there is less air pressure in them than in the outside atmosphere. When the diaphragm relaxes, the dome pushes up, the chest squeezes smaller, air pressure inside is greater than outside, and this causes the air to rush out.

A person will die if his or her breathing stops for four to six minutes.

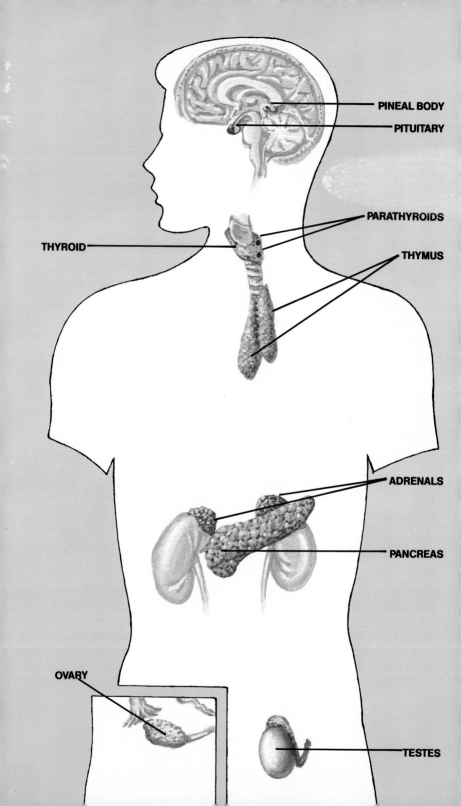

PINEAL BODY

PITUITARY

PARATHYROIDS

THYROID

THYMUS

ADRENALS

PANCREAS

OVARY

TESTES

GLANDS

A *gland* is an organ that produces specialized chemical substances used by the body. For example, digestive juices, tears, and sweat are made by glands. *Hormones* are substances made by glands that are carried to other parts of the body in the bloodstream. Hormones are chemical messengers that tell organs what to do and when to work. They often work together with the nervous system to regulate and control body activities.

The *pituitary gland* is called the "master gland" because its hormones stimulate other glands. It is located deep inside the brain. Pituitary hormones regulate growth, reproductive organ development, smooth muscle activity, and other important functions.

The *thyroid gland* is located in the throat just below the "Adam's apple." Its hormones affect growth, heart rate, body temperature, and other functions. The *parathyroids* are next to the thyroid. They regulate bone growth, muscles, and nerves.

Two *adrenal glands* (one on top of each kidney) secrete *adrenaline*. Adrenaline is the hormone that gets your heart pumping faster when you need to go into action.

Insulin is a hormone produced by the pancreas, a gland found behind the stomach. Insulin controls the amount of sugar in your blood.

The *ovaries* in females and *testes* in males are glands that affect appearance and reproduction.

The functions of the *thymus* and *pineal* glands are not yet completely understood.

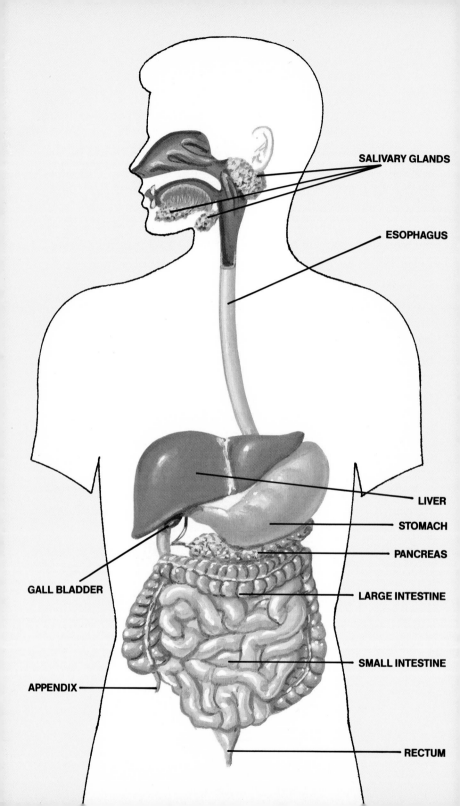

SALIVARY GLANDS

ESOPHAGUS

LIVER

STOMACH

PANCREAS

GALL BLADDER

LARGE INTESTINE

SMALL INTESTINE

APPENDIX

RECTUM

THE DIGESTIVE SYSTEM

Running, catching, and throwing require energy. Your body gets energy by burning sugars and fats in its cells. Sugars and fats come from the food you eat. An average person eats about a half ton of food each year.

Digestion changes food into materials the cells can use. The organs of your *digestive system* are the mouth, esophagus, stomach, small intestine, and large intestine.

Cells are tiny chemical factories. They convert raw materials in food into substances the body can use to produce energy. The raw materials first must be broken down into simple chemicals. The process starts in the mouth.

Food is chewed and mixed with saliva in the mouth. You make about a half quart of saliva a day. Swallowing forces the softened food down the esophagus and into the stomach where it stays from two to six hours. Strong digestive juices are added as the stomach churns the food into liquid. The liquid enters the small intestine where it is broken down into nutrients—carbohydrates (sugars and starches), fats, and proteins. The small intestine is about 20 feet long.

The lining of the small intestine is covered with a velvety covering of *villi*. Nutrients and water in the intestine are absorbed into the bloodstream through the villi walls and are carried to cells where they are used or stored.

Most nutrients are absorbed by the time the digested material reaches the large intestine. This material and other waste products are held in the lower part of the large intestine for elimination.

Food takes from 12 to 24 hours to be completely digested.

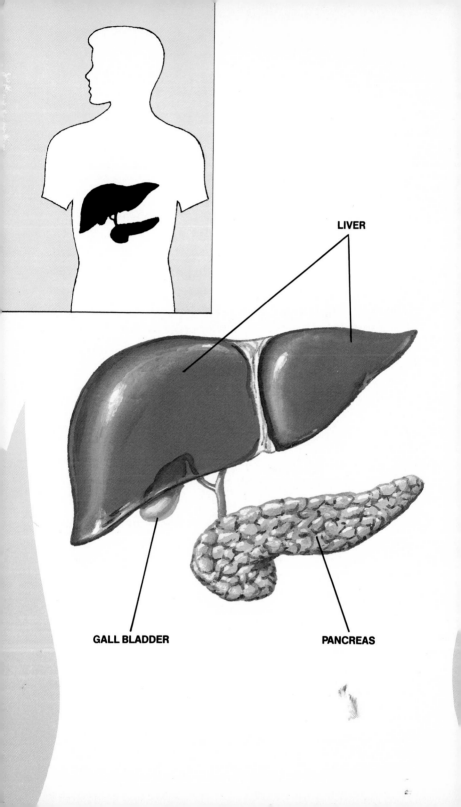

LIVER

GALL BLADDER

PANCREAS

THE LIVER, GALLBLADDER, AND PANCREAS

Digestion is aided by three specialized organs, the *liver*, the *gallbladder*, and the *pancreas*.

The *liver* is one of the body's most complicated organs. It has over 500 jobs. It is located next to the stomach, beneath the diaphragm. About a quart and a half of blood enters the liver every minute through its double blood supply. One supply brings oxygen-rich blood from the lungs. The other brings digested nutrients and raw materials the liver needs to do its many jobs.

The liver's main jobs are to store *glucose* (simple sugar), manufacture blood products, treat waste products, change fats so they can be used, make bile, remove poisonous materials from the blood, and make the material that prevents blood from clotting inside the circulatory system. The liver is a true chemical factory.

The *gall bladder* is a small, muscular sac behind the liver. It stores *bile* made by the liver and releases it as needed. Bile helps to break down fats in digestion.

The *pancreas* is a gland. It makes a strong digestive juice that helps to break down food in the stomach. It also produces *insulin*, a substance that is released into the blood to regulate the body's use of sugar.

The *appendix* is a finger-size extension of the large intestine. It may have aided digestion many thousands of years ago, though its exact job is not known. *Appendicitis* is an inflammation of the appendix.

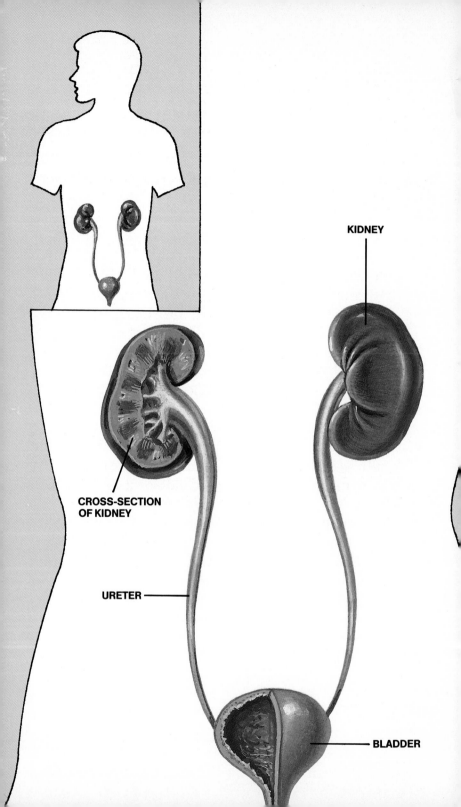

KIDNEY

CROSS-SECTION
OF KIDNEY

URETER

BLADDER

URINARY SYSTEM

Burning nutrients for energy, building tissue, and other body activities produce waste material the body must eliminate. Many body systems get rid of wastes. The digestive system eliminates *feces* (solid wastes and water) from the large intestine. The respiratory system eliminates carbon dioxide and water in the breath. The skin eliminates water and some waste salts in sweat. The *urinary system* removes waste products from the blood and eliminates them from the body in the urine.

You have two bean-shaped *kidneys,* one on each side, in the middle of your back. They are like filters and remove waste material from your blood. Each kidney has a *ureter* (tube) connecting it to the *urinary bladder*. The bladder is a sac for collecting urine. When the bladder is full, nerves stimulate the urge to empty it by urinating. Urine passes from the bladder to the outside through another tube, the *urethra*.

The kidneys also help the body to keep the right amount of water it needs to stay healthy. An average person is made of about 60 percent water. Cells are mostly water and so is blood. Much of the water is lost through elimination. To stay healthy, the lost water should be replaced by an equal amount of water in foods and drinking water. When it is not replaced, the kidneys help to regulate the water already in the body.

You get thirsty when the thirst control center in your brain senses you need more water.

An average person takes in about two and a half quarts of water a day. About one half comes from drinking water and beverages and the rest is in foods.

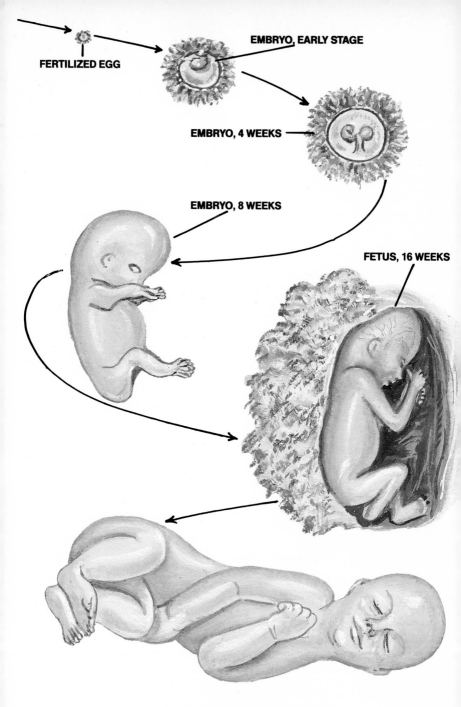

FERTILIZED EGG

EMBRYO, EARLY STAGE

EMBRYO, 4 WEEKS

EMBRYO, 8 WEEKS

FETUS, 16 WEEKS

FETUS, 38 WEEKS, READY TO BE BORN

THE REPRODUCTIVE SYSTEM

All living things are able to reproduce themselves. In animals, specialized cells from a male and a female are needed to produce offspring. Male reproductive cells, called *sperm*, are produced in glands called *testes*. Female reproductive cells, called *eggs*, are formed in the *ovaries*.

In human females, an egg takes about one month to mature. It leaves the ovary and enters the top of the *uterus*, a muscular organ in the lower part of a woman's abdomen. The walls of the uterus have a rich supply of blood vessels. If a sperm contacts the mature egg, fertilization occurs. A single cell is formed that contains information about both the father and the mother. Characteristics such as a person's size, shape, skin, eye, and hair color are just a few of the many thousands of bits of information carried in his or her parents' reproductive cells.

The fertilized cell attaches to the wall of the uterus where it is nourished by nutrients carried in the mother's blood supply. The cell immediately begins to grow. In about three months the growing offspring, called a *fetus*, resembles an infant. In about nine months the fetus is fully developed and ready to be born.

Fraternal twins occur when two separate mature eggs are fertilized. Fraternal twins have individual characteristics. One may be tall, with dark hair, and the other short, with light hair, for example.

Identical twins result when one fertilized egg divides and each half develops into a separate offspring. Identical twins have the exact same characteristics.

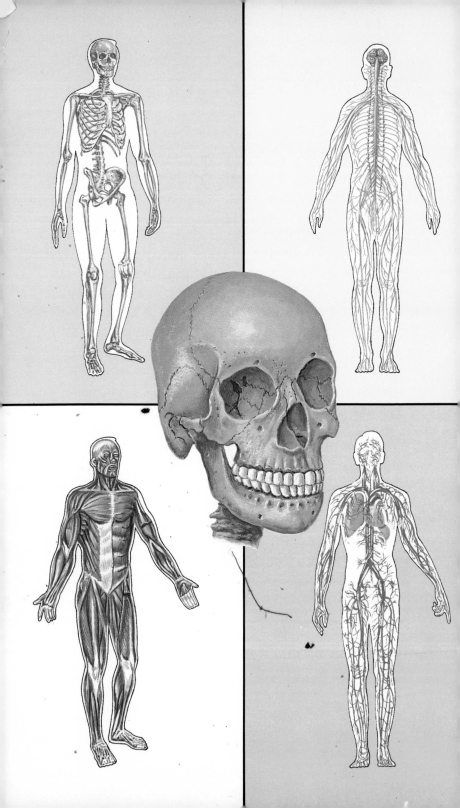